Donald Robinson Presents

Unleashing The Freak Within

Hot, Wet And Seductive

Table of Contents:

1. KeKe (My Angel)
2. You
3. Holding Her Gently In My Arms
4. I Close My Eyes And Your Beautiful Face Appears
5. I'M Your Fool
6. Lock And Key
7. Love Got Me
8. Can You Feel Me
9. No Sweet Lines
10. Pleasure
11. Secret Garden
12. Tonight I Am Going To Be Your Love Maestro
13. Undressing You With My Eye
14. Whenever Forever
15. Day Dreaming
16. 24 Hours Of Romance
17. A Million Days
18. Your Love Is The Ultimate
19. Can You Feel Me, Part 2.
20. Let's Not Move Too Fast
21. Lost In Your Love For An Eternity

22. My Love for You Burns Stronger Than Fire
23. My World Is Empty Without You
24. So Many Nights
25. This Is Not a Game
26. to My Love
27. When I Found Love
28. You Put a Spell on Me
29. Your Personality Clearly Speaks For It Self
(Intermission) Get The Ice, Whip Cream, Strawberries, Toys And Champagne
30. After Dinner and the Movie
31. When We Leave the Club
32. Chocolate Covered Strawberries and Cherries
33. Thickness
34. Dominican Love
35. Her Legs Open Wide
36. I Don't Want To Make Love
37. I Want To Get To Know You
38. Some Extra Freaky Shit
39. Making Love in the Shower
40. Role Play Foreplay
41. Sexual Dream
42. Sexy Slim Girl
43. She Made It Rain All Over My Face
44. She Told Me to Release It in Her Mouth
45. Thinking of You
46. Dedicated To MY Chocolate Girl
47. Touch Your Self
48. Mesmerized
49. Until The Room Is Full Of Steam And Our Bodies Are Hot And Wet.
50. laying with My Angel

Treat your Queen as the Diamond she is
So that she will always stay by your side
Do things to her that no other man can do
Make her always feel wanted and special
Feed her mind, body and soul the unconditional
Love she need's want's and deserves.

Day Dreaming:

I visualize you wearing a stimulating gown,
Light brown, soft skin
Beautiful long jet black hair dropping below your slender waist,
Smile exquisite as a rainbow,

You and I pleasantly walk hand in hand along the shore,
While love takes us on a romantic journey;
Holding you in my arms, our hearts begin to silently speak,
Your kiss soothes me like the morning breeze,

The fragrance of your sexy tender body pleases me,
As your eyes glisten with life causing my love for you to naturally overflow;
Your lips delicately kiss my neck,
The shadow of your love warms my soul,
While resting my head upon your breast,

Joy is what I feel when you and I are together,
Baby girl, you are the true meaning of peace;
I promise to never harm you,
Nor interrupt the everlasting bond you and I share,

Because it's not easy finding a woman who's honest,
Understanding, fair, and wise,
I just want you to know how I feel,
And what I see when I close my eyes when day dreaming of you.

Holding her gently in my arms
Feeling the warmth of the sun as it slowly begins to rise

I look into her delicate beautiful eyes
Only to witness the truth

Because her heart is too peaceful to carry wickedness
What a blessed man I am to have such a loving, devoted young lady

She hold not one drop of negativity
Because she comes from a family and environment that is 100% positive

I love her in more ways than one
My love for her is unexplainable

Day after day growing deeper and deeper
Strengthening the unbreakable bond that we share

She will always be my queen
Until I no longer exist

There's not a woman on this Earth who can ever take her place
Or do the things that she does

And even if there is it doesn't matter
Because I am dedicated to her
She will always be my one and only love

I close my eyes and your beautiful face appears,

That sexy smile puts me into a deep trance,

I just want to hold you close to my heart and slow dance,

Every moment spent with you is magical,

Right now I want to kiss your sweet soft lips, lay you down on the bed, and gently please your tender body,

You are honestly more than sexy, you are indescribable,

How can any man deny you?

My mind wanders as I envision the two of us having exotic hot sex in the bedroom,

I'll be the boy, who plays with you, the man to fulfill your every need,

I'll be that dude who will rough ride you, giving it to you raw until your scream out my name, begging me to stop, please, please, please,

And after I put in work and you whisper in my ear, "job well done," I'll hold you in my arms, run my fingers through your hair, and caress your mind with soothing words, until all your fears permanently disappear.

I'm Your Fool

The things I go through over you are just crazy,

But day after day your love seems to amaze me,

I've been loving you since the days of school,

The nonsense I let you do just 'isn't cool,

I love you so much,

I'm your fool…

I know you're not being true to me,

You're poisonous and as vicious as a bee,

How you're hurting me, I wish you could see,

I feel like drowning in a pool,

Because, I'm your fool…

So many times I pack my bags to leave and go away,

But somehow I let you convince my silly ass to stay,

I'm so stressed my hair is turning grey,

Today's important, Jewel,

I must stop being your fool…

Keke (My Angel)

My gift to you is constant pleasure,

Although the sun will not always shine,

You and I must remain bound together,

Because through it all, Love, you are forever mine;

If someone were to ever say loving you is a crime,

Then I plead guilty with a smile,

Because I refuse to be without you,

How can I breathe?

Love look at what it can do to a man,

The simplest things,

Just feels so good running my fingers through your beautiful hair,

Kissing you until my knees get weak,

Or just gently holding your little soft hand;

What you and I share is endless?

Just look into my eyes and see that our love is real,

Touch my heart so you can understand how I feel;

Do you need me, like I need you?

Our love can never be replaced,

Every time I look at you,

I learn more of the meaning of a true beautiful black woman,

And all she stands for.

Lock and Key

My brown skin,
Beautiful Queen,
So soft and tender,

Remember that hot summer day in the park where you and I met,
I believe it was the month of September,
Your eyes, still the same as they were then,
Innocent, loving, and hypnotizing,
Always making me surrender.
 Your soft skin is soothing my mind,

As I hold you in my arms, watching the rain silently fall,
We ran home to cuddle in front of the fire place,
Enjoying the quiet storm,
Our bodies filled with pleasure and peace,
Feeling, cozy and so warm.

Mentally and physically loving you in many ways,
Night and day,
You're constantly on my mind,
I guess my mother was right,
A good woman like you is hard to find,

You're my shining star, the one who frees me from darkness,
My lips yearn to feel your delicious kiss,
Tell your father I'm sorry for stealing his little princess,
 No matter where I may be, when you call me,
I will be there,

I'm confident no one can love you the way I do,
The love I hold for you in my heart is eternally true,
It's hard to explain how you make me feel,
These emotions are so strong,
I can't hide the bond we share as friends,
And as lovers, we are too real.

 You're sweet as honey in my tea,
Every time I close my eyes, your gorgeous face is all I see,
What kind of man would I be if I were to break your heart or leave you lonely?
Baby doll, without you there's no me,
You are the lock and I am the key…

Can You Feel Me?

Loving you is my law,
I have loved you from the start,
I will love you until my life ends,
Trials and tribulations have let me know,
Our love is real,

And you will always be on my side,
I'm in love with you, truly,
Can you feel me…?
You're my friend, love, and wife,
Every day spent with you is new life,

No matter what hard times we face,
You will always remain the same true, loyal, tender, lady,
Your beauty and kindness amazes me,
I don't want to waste our years on fighting,
Unnecessary tears, anger, and nightmares,
Can you feel me…?

With my eyes till closed,
I see us making love in front of the fireplace,
Until the energy has evacuated our bodies,
As we lay by the warm fire,

You gently lay your head on my chest,
We hugged and kiss,
I'm thinking to myself how I want you some more,
You're my desire,
You lift me up higher,
This distance between us is killing me,
I feel you,
But, can you feel me….

No sweet lines,

I'm not purposely trying to be smooth,

I promise that these words I speak are coming from my heart,

Honestly, I can't stand us being apart

Don't want love to fade away,

Because my world has no life without you

I go to bed broken down,

Because you are not around,

Missing your warm touch and soft voice,

God, have mercy,

Please spare me and my baby another chance.

Life is too short for us,

To let our relationship end in such a negative way,

By your side is where I must be,

You and I are a perfect fit,

Like lock and key,

Love, come back to me

Pleasure

Some may ask what is it? Or does such a great feeling truly exist? I say yes, pleasure is soothing to one's mind, body, and soul.

Just as my wife delights and excites me, the pleasure my angel feeds my heart makes me want to shout out and lose control.

When I look into her beautiful brown eyes, run my fingers through her hair, and caress her sexy chocolate skin, I receive pleasure.

It could be something as simple as holding hands while strolling through the park, enjoying dinner and a movie, calling one another during our lunch break, maybe even sharing a piece of cake gives me so much pleasure.

To watch you gently sleep after making your delicious body weak from sexing you down from head to toe, leaving you feel like Jamie Fox, unpredictable because the way I love you is incredible, and what I treasure is giving my angel nonstop pleasure.

Tonight I am going to be your love maestro,

The way my fingers will play with your body is guaranteed to excite you,
Watch how I tease you as I slowly bight you.
I am going to make love to you with perfection,
Check how I how I initiate this romance as I begin to examine,
That beautiful treasure inside your pants.
You're beauty has gotten my full attention,

Body posture showing off the sexiest attitude as you begin to free yourself,
And get nude,
Feel my lips flirt with your breasts,
While I work my way down to the middle, giving you my ultimate test,
Unwrapping your legs with my tongue,
Causing you to get hot and wet,

I can tell by the look in your eyes that I got you hypnotized,
You want to know how and why I got you feeling this way,
Sorry ma, it's an ancient black man secret,
Your gentle touch has an unbelievable influence over me,
The way your lips captivate my soul,
Really makes a brother lose control.

The warmth of your breast sooths my chest,
As I slowly push my pipe deep inside your mainline,
Giving you every drop of manpower as I flip it on you, I hit it from behind until the final hour,
You know how you like it rough because you think you're tough,
But I got news for you shorty,
I'm not going to stop until you scream pop, that's enough
I have to represent and let you feel the power of the Love Maestro….

Undressing You with my Eyes
Eyes locked on your body as if I had x-ray vision,
Thinking of ways I can please your precious temple;

As you let your hair down,
Slowly my lips begin to massage your tender neck,
Holding you in my arms lost in paradise,
Wow, this feels really nice.

Hands rubbing you up and down unbuttoning your blouse,
Unstrapping your Victoria Secret bra,
Taking off your skirt, causing both our body temperatures to rise,
You want me I can see it in your eyes.

My mission is almost complete,
Let's not forget those sexy red panties,
Oh I'm sorry, I mean sexy red thong.

Damn girl, I hope you're prepared for some real sexual action and satisfaction,
Now off comes the thong, Look at you lying on the bed,
So delicious and sweet, Open up your legs and let daddy eat.

When Ever For Ever

I love you whenever…Forever There was so much I wanted to say and so much you needed to say. There were many conversations between us. So much love we shared whenever forever…

Knowing that I love you and you love me, knowing that I miss you and you miss me. Whether you and I are far apart or close together whenever…forever…Whether times are good or bad, whenever…forever…. Knowing that when you hurt I hurt, knowing that I will always be here for you and you will always be here for me.

Knowing that I care for you with all my heart and you care for me with all your heart, understanding that our friendship could never be broken because what you and I share is priceless, whenever…forever.

Knowing that I understand you and you understand me, no matter how much we try to hide our emotions or feelings the small details tell me when you are happy or sad, whenever…forever…

Knowing that you will always be my queen and I'm your king, regardless if the tides are rough or smooth, whenever…forever…Knowing that I have given you strength and you have given me

Strength to make our days easier to deal with. Trusting that you and I will always be faithful and loyal to one another, feeding each other's hearts the unconditional love we need and deserve whenever…forever…

You …

Sitting here thinking about you, saying to myself she's so beautiful right about now. I wish you were here. I'd throw this pen and pad down so fast and kiss you all over your sexy tender body.

I'm going to celebrate every day because you are in my life. It's crazy, but baby girl, I can see you and me as husband and wife. Yeah, that's deep, I know, but you melt my heart like the warm sun melts snow.

Every phone conversation and moment spent with you is deeply cherished. Every kiss, hug, and little touch makes me cling to you tighter and tighter. More and more I can feel myself becoming a sincere lover and not a fighter.

So I'm asking myself, and you as well, have I finally found my true love? Someone who will be in my corner no matter what occurs? Or the one who I make love to so good that it can still be felt the day after?

You are an inspiration to me. Because of you I can see clearer now. You're probably saying, "How can this be?" Simply because of the person that you are and from the bottom of my heart I truly thank you for opening up my eyes, mind, and heart to want the best out of life…

Love,

Pop

24 Hours of Romance

As the candles light the room,
The music is playing soft and low,
Causing the mood to become all so perfect and magical.
 Listen to the sound of the ocean,
While our bodies perceive the midnight breeze,
Your beautiful smile has got me begging,
Baby, please,
Baby, please,

My actions will show you just how much I care,
You're all the woman I want and need,
Open your love up to me,
And let me plant my seed inside of you,
You and I both know true love is hard to find.
We will make love to the North, South, East, and West,
I am going to put your skills to the test,
Until our bodies are hot, wet dripping with sweat,
And you scream out, No More,

Making this a night neither one of us will ever regret or forget.
Love so contagious,
Good gracious,
I want to catch every drop of it tonight,
You and I will share each moment,
As if it were our last,

Lay back and relax, and unwind as my tender words soothe your mind.
My hands delicately caress your breast,
As my tongue converses with your soft, sexy thighs,
No need to speak, Angel,

I see it in your eyes
We now realize that it's time to take this love affair o the next level.
Your lips began to gently kiss my neck.
As you feel the power of my shaft enter into your sweet pleasing pond.
I would be a liar to pretend that I want this night to end,
So let's make the best of this special night,
Because we may not be guaranteed another chance,
At 24 Hours of Romance.

For a million days and nights my love is what

I desire to give you.

Do you understand the meaning of?

Trust, honesty, happiness, and love?

Your beauty is unexplainable, just as

The kindness you have stored in your heart;

Waiting for my day at work to come

To an end so I can come home and enjoy

Hugging and kissing all over you;

Winter, spring, summer, fall, I promise

To love you continuously through every season;

It feels good to lie in the bed, play in your hair,

Gently massage your entire body, do those little

Things that excite your soul, like licking your

Cute belly button, softly kissing your neck, and

Nibbling on your ear, year, I know how it makes

You feel;

I just want you to know how you make

I feel and that I look forward to giving you

Eternal pleasure, every time you and I are together.

Can You Feel Me Part 2?

As I closed my eyes last night and began to formulate you in my mind,
I visualize us holding hands and walking on the beach,
The sun gently warming our bodies,
The wind softly moved your hair,
As I looked into your eyes, our lips slowly came together,
Pleasure filled our souls,

The love we have is so real and beautiful,
Last night I felt you in my arms,
And I just wanted to know when you dream about me,
As I dream about you,
Can you feel me?

Although you and I are temporarily apart,
My love for you continues to grow mentally and physically,
I have told you many times,
Nothing and no person can permanently separate us except
God himself,

You mean so much to me,
I can't even begin to explain how much,
But I feel the love, care, and honor I have for you deep in my heart,
You're my friend as well as my love,

I miss you and you miss me,
I feel you, can you feel me?
We have a special bond that's unbreakable,
We have overcome many trials and tribulations at times,
I know you wanted to walk away at times,
Just as I wanted,

Anger and frustration caused us to say and do things we did not mean to do,
But through God's blessings our love conquered the pain and fears,
This romance you and I share is ultimately transcending,
I wonder, can you feel me?

LET'S NOT MOVE TOO FAST:

Since you and I have been together our lives, days and
Nights have been very pleasant. Romance is in the air hugs
And kisses with you is a pleasure to share just let love take
It's course and let's not move too fast.
I want to grow with you and build a solid mature
Relationship that will be unbreakable, immovable and we
Can do it we must take our time and not rush because I
Don't want to speed only to crash and lose your love.
Let us not lose control of our emotions or this beautiful
Bond you and I share the most important thing is that we
Trust, respect, and love one another in the right way and we
Can do that by keeping GOD in our lives in a part of our
Relationship.
We are happy right now so let's continue this happiness by
Always communicating especially when problems do occur
Because I don't like fighting or going to bed angry I want to
Love you for the rest of my life so let's not move too fast.

Lost in your love for an eternity.

You send peace into my life without you I really don't know where I would be.

You and I are like hand and glove, lock and key I am for you and you are for me.

We must keep our love pure at all times even through the roughest moments;

No matter what trials and tribulations you and I face, together or individually.

The key to a successful relationship and strong happy marriage is that we cannot let love fail.

Look into my eyes and you will see that these words I speak are sincere.

So many times I thought I knew what love was about but honestly since you have been in my life day after day I discover the meaning of true love.

That's why it is only right I take you by your tender little hand and ask you to be my wife.

My love for you burns stronger than fire

To kiss your sweet lips and look into your

Pretty eyes are what my heart constantly desires;

This is more than just talk,

If there is anyone here truly in love

Than I am sure he or she understands how I feel

And knows what I am talking about;

You were sent to me by prayer, faith, and patience

So I must keep our love peaceful

And handle you with care at all times;

You and I may not always see things the same way,

And I'm sure we can aggravate one another at times

But it's alright because through it all we always manage to build

We take our love higher and make the bond we hare stronger

As the days go by;

Love that feeling you get insider, can't really explain it,

But just got your face glowing and flowing all through your body from head to toe

The kind of love you never want to lose but continuously grow;

As long as you stay true to me, I will love you whenever, for whatever, Forever

And I assure you my love will always be as a never ending fire for you keeping

You secure and warm at all times.

My world is empty without you.

There is no war I wouldn't get into to protect you.

We are destined for true love. All that I have and will receive I'll be yours. There was a time my thoughts were constantly dreaming for hopes of you, a real woman so pure.

God told me to be patient and before I could blink my eyes twice, appeared my queen, who I search for no more.

A life time of nonstop hugs, kisses, loving, touching and endless love making is

All I want to share with you to wake up to the sun shining upon your beautiful

Face and gorgeous body how attractive you are and all so alluring.

Honestly I meant it when I tell you my world is empty without you

All I want to do is share every second of happiness with you no matter where we

Maybe or what we are doing as long as I am with you I know it's right and I am where I am supposed

To be.

SO MANY NIGHTS:

So many nights I have yearned for your touch; I miss you in the worst way and I can't wait to see you're lovely Face; I love you and all that you stand for I appreciate the love you Express to me the absence of your affection lets me know how Much you mean to me and where I want to be when I come home Because in here I am cold alone and hurt as the lights click off I Prepare myself for another lonely night.

So many nights I want to hold you in my arms kiss you from head To toe feel the warmth of you, play in your hair please you, tease You and excite you. I wish to bless your mind and body with Kindness, sincerity and devotion I want to enjoy your Companionship tasting your sweet love which takes me to ecstasy I Praise you so many nights.

So many nights tears drop from my eyes feeling nothing but pain And loneliness I never thought we would be apart like this I close My eyes to feel your kiss because just maybe this pain will end but Emptiness is all I receive at times I lose my thoughts because I am In this hole hurting so many nights.

This Is Not a Game

This is not a game, two hearts

Should be together, but what happened

Why do they remain separated?

That beautiful smile of yours I should

Be seeing it daily feeling the warmth of

Your sweet love should be all mines;

Love is confusing, at times it can make

One feel lost but every time I look into

Your eyes I am found;

Mentally, you and I are

Inseparable and I know if we were to

Ever become physical it would be also

Incredible because to me you have always

Been special;

Sometimes when I look at you I want

To immerse my magic wand into you and put

You in a never ending trance but somehow I

Believe we missed our chance at romance…

To My Love:

You are the definition of a True woman

In my eyes you are the greatest, everything about you is perfect

So please don't you ever change;

It is not easy finding that special one to call your queen

Someone to share your dreams and goals with,

To laugh, cry or stay by one's side when the tides get rough,

Your ways and actions show me time and time again that

You are more than my friend.

Yes I have found a friend in you that cannot be found

Anywhere else on

This planet and for that I cherish you deeply,

You and I will walk together hand in hand until the end

Of time. And with all of my heart I promise to

Give you eternal happiness making every day spent

With you filled with romantic memories.

Husband and wife forever, your love is priceless

Your beautiful mind, body and soul I will always protect

Treasure and respect your heart I will.

When I found love,

I knew it was true,
Although I had not a clue,
The things love would make me do.
I have no regrets for the things love has made me experience,
Because I was able to learn what love is about to strengthen me,
I appreciate all that you do.

When I found love, I was just a lonely man,
Searching for romance,
A friend and lover,
Then God sent me,
You and no more did I have to look for happiness,
My heart once was weak, but you made it strong,
And at times I know I've been wrong,
But you never gave up on me,
For this I love you, truly.

When I found love,
I was so honored just as I am today,
And I promise to make you happier each day,
I will take away your pain, fears, and dry your tears,
With you I pray to be with for many years,
I bless the heavens from up above because when I found you I found love.

You Put a Spell on Me:

Your passion, devotion, and tenderness has got me hypnotized,
I never knew romance could feel this good
Every time I'm around you my body gets hot as an oven,
Drown me with your tender loving.

I can never get enough of your sweet love,
Women are jealous and angry because I won't leave you,
Many men want to know why I love you the way I do,
Damn, baby girl, only if they knew the things I know,
What can I say except, you're incredible.

As w being to physically express our love,
My hand gently caresses your breast,
I hear you softly whisper, lower and lower,
And in your peaceful garden I find pleasure and rest.

I promise to never leave you lovely,
What the hell is going on,
You got me going crazy,
Your love lifts me higher than L.S.D.,
Sexy lady, you put a spell on me…

Your Love Is The Ultimate:

Alone in my room,

I sit dreaming of you,

Thanking God for your love, friendship, and encouragement,

You're all the woman I ever need and want,

Day after day our bond continues to grow stronger,

The pleasure you give to me is unexplainable,

But so incredible.

I will never cause your heart pain,

A lifetime of happiness is what you deserve,

I'm proud to say to the world that you are my sexy queen,

With me by your side,

You have nothing to worry about,

I will be your sunshine when problems come your way.

I see am smile always on your face,

Soothes my soul,

I enjoy the sweet taste of your lips,

I love you form the north, south, west, and east,

Your skin is so tender and delicate,

Your gorgeous body is my feast,

My love for you is factual, because your love is The Ultimate.

Your personality clearly speaks for everything you are,

What you and I share goes deeper than love,

Sometimes I can't explain my thoughts or my feelings,

But I know in my heart that you will always be without a doubt,

The one I shall eternally adore,

You are the flower that completes the garden.

What you and I share, is priceless

It's deeper than love.

The bond that you and I share is unexplainable

But I feel it in every kiss, touch and all the special moments

That you and I share each and every day.

Your character defines you as a true lady

It's in the way you represent yourself

The way you walk, talk and smile.

You are the greatest woman I know

So please do not ever change

I love you, and always will love you

In every way possible until the Good

Lord calls me home and even then I

Pray my love touches you from

Heaven so that you know I am remain

With you and still in love with you.

After Dinner and the Movie:

I am going to take you home and light some scented candles just how you like,

And I will play your favorite slow jams to comfort you and set the mood,

Relax and let me slip off your sandals and massage your pretty feet slowly bringing a warm sensational feeling to your body as I begin to fully undress you and gently kiss your body over and over as I whisper all the correct words you like to hear.

Now your body is hot and moist ready for love and not just your ordinary love, you and I will engage in an undeniable, uncontrollable special kind of love until both of our bodies are joyfully weak can barely speak the only thing we will be able to do is lay still in a trance.

Maybe I'll hand cuff you and blind fold you spread your legs apart and let my tongue and face sink deep into your sweet pond and touch your favorite spot as many times as I possibly can causing you to climax multiple times and then I will take the handcuffs and blind fold off and turn you over just as you like and begin to push my magic wand inside of you getting freakier smacking that ass pulling your hair talking nastier and nastier letting you know I am the only man who can please your mind body and soul.

And I am sure to have you smiling ear to ear every time I treat my Baby to dinner and a movie because you will know and understand what our special dates entail because I am all about romancing you, loving you and spoiling you make you feel as a woman deserves. It's always a pleasure to be your special desert After Dinner and the Movie.

When we leave The Club

Just came in from the club it's about 2 A.M. I'm saucy feeling the henny run through my veins my wife is like what you want to do I give her that look and tell her Take it all off stripping her clothes up until she ass naked then she peels of my clothes and I lay her on the bad lick her up and down getting her extremely wet so wet I know the sheets going to have to come up off this bed right now she got me in the zone from the mind blowing head oh shit it's going down tonight up in here.

I pull her legs up in the air over my shoulders and work that pussy just the way she likes pleasing her body until the point of no return she tells me I want to ride that dick so she gets on top of me and starts moving up and down in a slow motion asking me you like that Daddy I look her in the eyes and tell her do that shit baby grabbing and sucking her chocolate titties smacking her ass as she begins to move a bit faster.

See this is the type shit I be on when I leave the club with wifey both of us can't wait to get home to keep the night going just on another kind of level no love making tonight we going to break the bed up in this mother fucker we going to disturb the neighbors on some real shit they know my name when they hear my baby moaning and screaming give it to me Pop.

Loving my chocolate Angel in so many ways making all of her sexually fantasies com true tonight I am going to show just what it is what my tongue and dick can do. Romance and Pleasure is my confession brace yourself for this love lesson as I gently push this strawberry in and out of her licking her sweet juices off it with my tongue spreading her legs further apart pushing deep inside of her whispering dirty things in her ear as she grabs me tight digging her nails in my back never feeling a damn thing because I am zoning out as I go deeper inside of her enjoying every bit of her wetness

 I lean her over the bed pushing up in her from behind going ham on that pussy spanking her talking crazy letting her know it's mine she tells me don't stop give it to me let it explode all over my ass Daddy so I give her what her heart desires and as we lay there holding one another talking and laughing about our night enjoying the pleasure with my lover and friend she knows how we do when we leave the club

CHOCOLATE COVERED STRAWBERRIES AND CHERRIES: PT 1

Oh yeah it's me the irresistible poem writer, the one who's got you so suspicious because you heard through the grapevine that I am so nutritious and that I am the man who will give your body constant pleasure by all means.

So being that you're curious I figured you and I could dedicate ourselves to a night of CHOCOLATE COVERED STRAWBERRIES AND CHERRIES to enhance your dreams.

At least when your thoughts are on me so listen to my sexual plan!

Lay back and relax this is free of charge no tax with the 69 position included, let me melt into your body like hot wax; push this love affair to the max. CHOCOLATE COVERED STRAWBERRIES AND CHERRIES are a passion that's sweet I 'm delighted and you're invited to a treat cause I 'm hot like fire ready to erupt like a volcano and let my lava flow my body is yearning for you like a dog in heat.

Chocolate covered breast I confess you are the best as you place your tender caramel nipples in my mouth, hands slowly caressing those beautiful thighs, check how I flip it on you and take a trip down south. Intoxicated off the heavenly sensation leading you to penetration got you screaming my and I am not going to stop until I hear your body joyfully cry.

Tonight there will be no love making just strictly fucking I'm talking about that back breaking, head board hitting, bed shaking, pony tail pulling, ass slapping type of fucking the kind of love that will leave you curled up sucking your thumb as if you were a new born baby.

Mixing this chocolate with your cream is better than a vanilla sundae supreme you know the kind that's every real man's dream. So this is why I have to take it to the extreme, open your legs and feel me dive in between you're about to witness something never heard of or seen damn shorty your pussy got me hooked like a Fein.

Surrounded by strawberries and cherries no questions asked only sessions of exotic hot sex contemplating on what I am about to do next, rich thick chocolate dripping off of you tasting so good my sexy freak don't get it misunderstood because this love affair feels so good. And I 'm feeling the way you work that cherry with your lips as you pour that creamy chocolate on my dick catching it with your tongue before it touches my balls tongue so damn dangerous you got my head bouncing off the walls.

Feeling the way you greet my dick with great pleasure so it's only right I give it to you in every measure feel loves pressure because after tonight you will have become my permanent treasure, and I am not going to stop until daddy hears his little mommy screams she sees the light yeah shorty its going down like that.

Putting this love affair on delay would only cause me a valuable price to pay so act like you know and have it your way. I got a milk shake for you that's better than your favorite ice cream the protein I got for you is necessary you know the kind that will keep you warm all through the month of February I 'm going to smoke you like some good old purple haze lick your body up and down leave you in a daze bless your temple with an ultimate spark and blaze.

Pushing deeper inside you moving faster and faster like a run away money train my love flows through your body like the blood in your veins you got me open truly hypnotized off of the doggy style position as I slide my dick into your round soft juicy ass moving with a slow motion giving you my magic potion enjoying the feeling of sexual healing never losing concentration never hesitating on causing you to reach you r peak make your delicious body incredibly weak.

I 'm sure to have you saying he's a hell of guy for real no lie, CHOCOLATE COVERED STRAWBERRIES AND CHERRIES IS shared only between you and I so amateurs please no need to try, CHOCOLATE STRAWBERRIES AND CHERRIES spread all over you boo this is what real experienced lovers do, remember always I love you.

I am checking Mama out and she knows it
I see how she keeps watching me looking at her
But I can't help it she is just thick in all the right places
Damn if she only knew how I would turn her sexy ass out.

For instances I would take her back to my place
And strip her down until she was completely naked
Then relax with her in my hot tub playing all the right music that would

Get her in the mood to be loved like she has never been loved before
Oh you want to see what my tongue can do
Well let me lay you on this bed face down
So I can lick that pussy from the back and then
Tickle the crease of your ass with my tongue I'm a freak

So yes I am going to lick that ass inside and out I'm just saying
This is how I enjoy pleasing my thick girl
You like how I grab and squeeze your delicious titties with a
Bit of roughness and suck your nipples until they are incredibly hard
And your body temperature begins to rise

Get on top of my dick and ride it with it slow motion
you know how I like it ride that wood in an insane type of way
get loud and wild until you wet it all let your sweet juices run down on me

Now I'm getting freakier let me put my face in it and lick and suck
away as you tremble with so much pleasure,
I enjoy watching you place my dick in your
Mouth and you lick it up and down rubbing it
all over your face then forcing it back in your mouth
sucking and licking it until I explode but where not finish yet

You tell me to get behind your thick delicious ass and hit it from the back
You whisper fuck me hard and spank my ass like a naughty girl
so I give you what you want and fuck you like a nasty girl
you grab me and suddenly pull my dick
Out of your pussy holding it in your hand asking
me do I want a treat from you I say yes
you tell me to hold on tight because you are about to make it bounce

Then you slowly begin to push my dick in your soft thick ass
I grab on to your thighs as you begin to move back and forth
bouncing that ass like a chic in the strip club
Got me ready to spend some money
You tell me give it to you harder and harder faster and faster

I am going all out satisfying you just as you deserve pulling your ponytail
Riding that ass never slipping out talking dirty to you
Just how you like it then I feel it at the top
Oh shit I'm Cumming you pull my dick out and say
Let it bust all over my thick chocolate ass you lay quiet in pleasure
and I look at you saying to myself
Damn these thick girls ,they know how to put it down.

Dominican Love:

I could never deny the beauty and love of a Dominican Woman dedicated and pure knowing just what it means to satisfy her man by any means necessary in a respectful manner;

Dominican love my heart yearns for you, as I reflect on how you and I make love and engage in romantic mornings, afternoons and evenings they are truly unforgettable;

To stay locked in your arms in where I rather be than anywhere else in the world the reason being is because you are my world and I love all that you stand for;

One thing I've learned for sure is that not all women are faithful but when a man finds that true Dominican Mommy he has hit the jackpot because she is going to ride strong with him until the end of time;

Some may think I am being bias and hate but it's whatever all I know is my Dominican queen will make you weak in the knees with her beautiful long hair pretty smile and sexy soft skin delicious hips and gorgeous hips;

I could go on and on about My Dominican love and all that she does and much of a great woman she is but it's not cool to brag I am thankful for her and she is thankful for me respect to my Dominican love and all the true honest Dominican women.

HER LEGS OPEN WIDE

After a long day of work I walk up to the door step inside and there she stands beautiful as always completely naked with sex in her eyes and passion in mine both of us very clear of what each other wanted.

There was no need for words or spoken desires... our body language said it all as she ripped off my clothes and dropped to her knees and with her long seductive beautiful tongue, she begin licking me up and down gently teasing and pleasing my dick with great delight.

I knew exactly what I wanted to do I was more than ready to please her so I flipped her over on the dining room table straight 69 session like there was no tomorrow she moaned and trembled with great pleasure then I switched positions and laid her on her back and begin to finger pop her while running my tongue up and down her clit and she kept screaming for more of that good shit.

She pulled me into the bedroom and started popping that ass making my dick even harder as I smacked that ass and bent her over playing with that pussy ... mama soaking wet she fell into a handstand and I watched her legs open wide, wide as the ocean and I jumped in for a swim and kept diving deeper and deeper.

As a bit of time passed by mama threw me on my back and started riding my waves ... I'm laying back enjoying it to the best of my ability as she bounced up and down staring at her soft round juicy ass until I lost control and nutted inside of her she then looks me in the eyes and says mama enjoys relieving daddies stress when he has had a long day of work.

I Don't Want To Make Love:

Tonight I am not making love to you instead I want nothing but exotic Fucking shared between you and I

Raw uncut sex for a few hours sounds like a beautiful plan so let's get freaky really get into it every and any position we can think of.

I want that head board banging, nasty talking, ass slapping, back scratching heavy breathing kind of fucking so don't hold back because I am going all in.

I want to eat your pussy and make you orgasm several times over and over again and then you can return the favor and suck my dick until I cum as much you make me cum.

I want to break the bed fall out of it and keep fucking on the floor make your body squirm and shake let you know how good daddies dick is.

Get on top of me and take control slam that pussy down on my dick uncontrollably letting me knows you got the best pussy on the planet.

And just when I think you had enough I want you to surprise me and say push in my ass and grab my titties and fuck me hard until you cum deep in my phat ass.

Yeah sometimes it has to be this way no love making just strictly exotic fucking.

I want to get to know you:

You are the kind of woman every man desires to be with, may I ask you your name and by chance if this conversation opens up the door for us to exchange numbers and which I hope it does because honestly I want to get to know you;

Every time you walk by I can't help but to stare and think to myself she is so beautiful and classy you appear to have that love I need a life time of being your lover, friend, protector and provider is what I would give you. I just want to get to know you;

What's it like to hold your hand and walk with you through the park enjoying every moment with you, your tender heart I would never hurt no matter what the days and night may bring all I want to is be the man you deserve to have the man that will always keep you strong and never let you get weak and fall I guarantee you that you and I will be forever.

You may feel that I am being bold but the truth is I may not get another chance to express my thoughts and these feeling that I have inside of me and no matter what happens after this talk you and I are having at least I know I told this attractive woman how I felt about her. Maybe we can meet here tomorrow and talk some more about what your interest in life are or I can extend an invitation to take you out to lunch or dinner because it would allow more time for me to get to know you yes I just want to get to know you.

First I am going to pick her up from work then drop her off at home so she can go in the house, shower and slip into something sexy and I will be back in 1 hour to get her;

Second she and I will go out to eat, her choice it's on me we can sit and talk over a delicious meal sip on some wine have a few shots of Patron until we start feeling a bit nice;

Third I will drive her down to the pier where we can sit and overlook the water enjoy the warmth of the moon and stars watching the boats sail in and out. Here is where we begin to set the mood by flirting with one another a little kissing, hugging and touching.

Four we will get into the car drive to a dark discrete place I will tell her to get out of the car and place her on the hood pull her panties off and raise her skirt up and proceed to lick and suck on her soft flesh until her orgasm and beg for more of my outstanding love;

Now that her body temperature is rising I see that she is ready because she takes her hand and gently starts to massage my dick making it intensely hard she pulls down the zipper to my pants and pulls my dick out and begins licking and sucking, moaning telling me how good it taste to her;

With a little aggression I turn her over into a doggy style position and passionately push my pipe into her tender hole feeling the tightness and wetness she begins to loosen up telling me to take my time and enjoy her;

she then tells me to go harder deeper and faster as we both unleash our freaky side I'm slapping that ass pulling her ponytail while she talks nasty to me and tell me to get this pussy its yours daddy take it punish me with that dick let me know it's yours, now I am going crazy all in car rocking and shaking letting her know that pussy is mine;

We pause for a moment roll the window down for some air holding her in my arms we begin to kiss and touch some more then she quickly sits on top of me and start moving up and down with a slow tempo looking into each other's eyes neither one of us thinking about stopping this incredible moment of hot sex she tells me to lay on my back as we place ourselves in the 69 position licking and sucking until we both reach our peak and climax;

Still not done she says to me let's get out of the car and fuck so we move to the back of the car where I have her leaned over the trunk arms and legs spread out she whispers fuck me good baby claim this pussy you are my king, lover and I need you to satisfy my inner freak. So I start to fuck her like a dirty slut she puts my hand around her neck and says choke me, fuck me like a nasty bitch I been a bad girl daddy and I need to be spanked and tamed.

I proceed to fulfill her wishes as we both climax again she says I want more, demanding me to put my dick in her ass telling me not to stop until she tells me to. you cum so again I must satisfy my freaky girl so I take my time handling her with gentleness, until she feels the need for me to go deeper she tells me baby don't hold back get in that ass so I start to go hard she says oh yeah like that get rough make me understand you're the boss enjoying every second of this exotic love session pounding her juicy ass I yell out I am Cumming she says pull out and let it splash all over my juicy ass so I do as she says and unleash my sperm all over her ass.

She turns to me and says now take me home and fuck me some more let's play our favorite game and role play I will be your dirty lil secretary and you be my irresistible boss I smile and agree to let her have her way sometimes this is what husband and wife have to do at times is get some extra freaky wild shit.

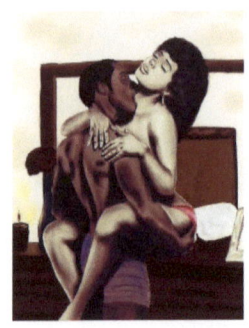

Mesmerized:

Many times she has passed me by always looking so lustrous,

It's clear to see that she is a true lady it shows in her character,

My eyes are locked on her as If I had ex ray vision thinking of ways I can please her precious temple,

As she lets her hair down slowly, my lips began to massage her tender neck while holding her in my arms lost in paradise… Wow this feels so good, really nice,

My hands begin rubbing her shoulders, back and thighs she pulls me close and kisses me I start to unbutton her blouse and unstrap her Victoria secret bra removing her dress with intentions to please her like no man has ever satisfied her before,

My mission is almost complete let's not forget to remove that sexy red thong damn girl you are so amazing I hope you're prepared for some real sexual action is what I say to her as she lays looking so beautiful across the bed she opens and closes her legs teasing me asking me do I want to her,

Suddenly she says hello how are you today I stutter and realize oh shit let me straighten up because this beautiful woman has got me mesmerized stuck on them thick delicious thighs.

Role Play Foreplay:

She enters into the room with her naughty maid's uniform on, looking so seductive and attractive teasing me as she slowly sticks out her tongue licking her lips;

She ask me what would I like to nibble on, I tell her my mouth is in the mood to taste something sweet she leans forward and gently pushes me back on the bed and unbuttons my shirt I attempt to touch her she says no let me do all the touching;

So I let the naughty maid have her way and take control, she unbuckles my belt and slides my pants to the floor using her mouth to pull down my boxer shorts then takes her lips and kiss me up and down my shaft before placing it in her mouth;

She tells me to demand her to feed me, so in a loud tone I order her to satisfy my appetite she pushes a pineapple in my mouth from her mouth delicately tasting my ear whispering to me that she is going to fuck me so good, I instantly open up her shirt and begin sucking her titties and licking her nipples;

She then lays back on the bed and tells me to watch her please herself so I sit back and enjoy the show as she starts to push her fingers inside of her pussy while with the other hand squeezing her tittie she tells me I want to see you play with your dick;

The mood now becoming more and more exciting I begin to stroke my dick up and down she moans and says in a freaky tone oh I like to watch you stroke your dick. My naughty maid begins to taste her own juices licking her fingers turning me on more and more she than tells me to stop stroking my dick and comes over to me and touches it she says Damn you're so hard and then she jumps on top and begins to ride;

She's grinding hard and deep I feel her wetness against my dick and it feels so good she then takes a strawberry and tells me to wet it with her juices and she wants me to eat it I do as my naughty maid says she is such a freak turned on by what I did she begins riding my dick faster and faster;

I turn my naughty maid over and begin to take a cherry and rub it up and down the crease of her ass as I kiss her juicy cheeks both of us hotter than a camp fire I tell my naughty maid to get into a 69 position and we engage in pleasing one another at the same time until we both release ourselves;

Bodies trembling and shaking due to the sensation of the ultimate sex but were not done yet by the look in our eyes it's clear that we both want more so I lay her on the bedroom floor and tell her to put her legs up in the air over my shoulders and I begin to pound her pussy making her climax again and again as we fall into a peaceful paradise of love our bodies unable to move she Finally speaks and says I love it when we role play and have foreplay with a smile on my face I tell her yes I enjoy it as well.

Making Love In the Shower:

Lying in bed holding each other kissing quickly getting in the mood to make love she says I have an idea she tells me to follow her to the bathroom and as we enter the bathroom she turns on the shower bringing the temperature to a comfortable feeling;

The water softly touches are bodies as we hold each other close kissing and soothing one another my hands caressing her thighs and breast sucking her nipples until they are hard arousing her and exciting her body;

I slowly drop to my knees spread her les apart and start to lick and suck the juices out of her wet pond she pulls my faces in closer causing me to push my tongue in deeper she says right there and begins to climax;

I then stand up and look at the heavenly look she has in her eyes she smiles back and then goes down on me pushing my shaft in her mouth giving me an erection that is out of this world she is moving her head back and forth licking me up and down and as I begin to ejaculate she pulls my shaft out of her mouth and let it explode all over face;

She then get up and turns around leaning over but pulling me close to her she says push it in I want to feel your big large shaft deep inside me so I push my love inside of her and we begin to engage in a mind blowing session of sex in the shower I spread her legs apart even more and now I'm banging that ass with all my power she's moaning loud telling me to give it to her and don't stop until I cum;

Suddenly she stops she says I am feeling very kinky she pulls me out of her leans over a bit further rubs my shaft on her ass and says I want you to fuck me in my ass she pushes my dick in her ass I begin to push in slow and deep until it's all the way in she tells me fuck me hard make me cum baby It turns me on to get fucked in the ass and to orgasm I proceed to give it to her just as she wants it pushing deeper moving back and forth with one of my hands gently around her waist the other hand spanking her moving faster and faster I tell her I am about to cum she pulls it out and I watch my shaft squirt all over her sweet juicy ass her body trembles because she has had an orgasm this is what it is to Make Love in the Shower.

Sexual Dream:

I can feel you kissing my lips and touching my body,
This is the moment you and I have been waiting for,
We begin to take off of our clothes,
Committing to a night of hot sex,

Tonight I'm going to physically express how much I care,
Your special spot I will be sure to reach
and without a doubt make you feel real good more than you can imagine,

Loving you is the only thing on my mind love is what you and I shall share,
Let's play a game of kiss and touch as I show you just how real I am,
As you look into my eyes I gently fondle your delicate thighs,
You whisper true romance never dies,
Holding a cherry in your mouth playing with it with your tongue
enticing me to take a trip down south,

You on to me and me on top of you,
There are so many things I am going to do to you,
You will be mesmerized head over heels for me,
How would you like if I licked some vanilla ice cream off of you,
Suddenly I hear someone calling me
but please don't wake me because I am enjoying this exotic
Intense Sexual Dream….

Sexy Slim Girl:

Her body feels so good,

My chest gently rest against her soft breast,

I run my fingers through her hair and kiss her everywhere,

Sexually I am going to show her just how experienced I am,

I am going to take her exactly where she is supposed to be when it comes to making love and pleasing her mind, body and soul,

Staring into her beautiful eyes caressing her thighs thinking about what I am going to do to her first as I flirt with her whispering charming words in her ear,

I undress her and place her on the bed and begin to strip naked also, I then pick her up and passionately kiss her lips and kneel down on my knees and kiss her belly button spreading my slim girl's legs slightly apart so I can put my face and tongue where she likes it,

Licking my slim girl until she gets wet I tell her don't be afraid relax and free herself because I want to love you all kind of ways so many lessons of love I am going to teach her by the time we are done she's guaranteed to be a pro,

We must make this night the best ever, candles light the room a little Keith sweat playing because I plan on making this night last forever, mood just right our body temperatures are rising I am enjoying how she gives it up in the bedroom,

Playing with a few of her favorite toys handcuffs, mini leather whip and some white wine my slim girl tasting the whip cream and strawberries on top of me slow grinding telling me to penetrate my love deep inside of her,

Her eyes roll back in her head she's clutching on to the sheets feeling the power of my shaft stroking her flesh in a way she understands I am not an amateur only a professional she tells me I am the best ever and I tell her she is my delicious slim girl so let it rain on me until she cannot rain anymore.

She Made It Rain All Over My Face:

I crave to taste her sweet juices, so I demand her attention and tell her there's a special treat I have been feigning for all day long;

Without hesitation I ask her to take off all her clothes she says no you take them off so I begin to take off her blouse and unbutton her jeans and releasing her out of her bra and panties now she's standing in front of me naked and all so beautiful as I stare at her I say to her I know exactly what I want;

She says to me baby do you want me? I respond yes I do, you are that fix I need so irresistible beyond belief sexy and seductive she tells me let me worship you whatever you want I will do;

We both lay on the bed ass naked touching, kissing, rubbing making the room steamy and hot I begin to feel her wetness as I caress her pussy with my hands;

I lay flat on the bed and pull her pussy all the way up to my face and she begins rubbing her pussy on my face in a slow motion but the more she gets wet she moves faster;

My tongue licking her clit up and down she starts to moan and grab the sheets screaming my name like she just heard it for the first time I'm eating her pussy with no shame tongue now deep inside of her touching her spot;

She starts to say oh shit oh shit right there her body starts to tremble with pleasure then suddenly she squirts her juices all over my face until she has no more to release I tell her yes sexy just like that all over my motherfucking face.

She told me to Release it in her mouth:

As I walk into the house she says to me I missed you and I have been thinking about you all damn day I ask her what she has been thinking about. She replies pleasing you in a way that you will surely enjoy.

She says to me, she has had a taste for me since I left this morning and she must satisfy her thirst and she truly wants me to quench it because she just can't get it off of her mind and that she must really have it.

I ask her what is it that she wants she says I want to suck your dick and taste every bit of your cum I instantly gain an erection to perfection she lays me on the couch and pulls my pants down and begins to caress my dick with her hands then her tongue and pushes it slowly in and out of her mouth her lips and tongue going to work on my dick in such a pleasurable way got me losing my mind;

She suddenly pulls my pants all the way off and open my legs apart still sucking on my dick caressing my inner thigh rubbing my balls with her soft hands she begins to go deeper gagging and swallowing telling me to fuck her mouth real good with my dick talking dirty telling me to explode in her fucking nasty mouth;

I lay in amazement of how she handles my fat dick in her mouth sucking slurping gagging and teasing it with her tongue she says I can taste it daddy cum in my fucking mouth turning me on by the nasty talk I begin to feel the volcano about to explode she says cum for me daddy please give me my cum I want to taste it so I grab her by her pony tail and pull her mouth down deeper I whisper oh fuck I feel it Cumming she says let it go daddy and suddenly I exploded in her mouth releasing my cum that she so badly wanted to taste.

Thinking Of You:

Thinking of you makes me want to taste your sweet lips hold you in my arms and mentally caress you in a way that no other man could ever do. Physically I will satisfy you to the point of no return only to have you repeatedly coming back for more of my love. Your smile is more beautiful than an calm ocean breeze the soft tone of your voice soothes my soul as I delicately run my fingers through your hair the chemistry shared between you and I is also powerful, magical something kind of unexplainable but one thing for sure it feels damn good.

When I am thinking of you it makes me want to do nice things like send you flowers or buy you a nice gift just because I want to make you smile and feel special let you know your loved. I never need to wait for a special time of the year to show you how much I care because loving you every day is what I am supposed to do it's what a real man does. I appreciate your never ending loyalty so it's only right I spoil you with unconditional love.

A Mental thought of you run's wild in my mind, I envision us making love in every position hugging, touching and kissing until our bodies get weak making the sex unforgettable. I enjoy your freaky side like when you want to go out in the back yard and get intimate in the rain or pulling over on the side of the road and get wild and crazy from the front seat to the back seat out on the hood of the car then take you home and sex you down some more. How would you like for me to make love to you over the moon light and stars or maybe down on the beach turn you out like Maestro Barry white until you Practice what you Preach.

Damn Baby when I am thinking of you these are just some of the thoughts that come to my mind.

This is dedicated to My Chocolate Girl (My Wife)

Allow me to share a few words with you this evening my love I think these are some things you need to hear.

I'm infatuated with your beautiful smile, soft sexy chocolate brown skin and those delicious lips, every time I hold you in my arms I never want to let you go because I cannot imagine myself without you this must be what heaven feels like because your love feels so damn delightful.

When I make love to my chocolate girl it's the greatest feeling I have ever felt sometimes I wonder if you really know how my soul melts into yours and our minds connect and the passion shared between you and I is a blessing from God.

My chocolate girl you're the one I desire to please until my last breath all I want to do is love you spiritually mentally as well as physically a love like ours is sure to last a life time I will love you like no other man can simply because I'm a real man who seeks to please his woman's heart by all means.

Chocolate girl My chocolate girl how about I run you a hot bubble bath and gently cleanse your sexy body from head to toe then dry you off and do some special things to you things that your heart enjoys.

You know how you love for me to lotion your soft skin from front to back and give you my famous massage that will lead to you and I making love you know how I like to let my hands journey all over you causing you to get excited in more ways than one.

My chocolate girl deserves to have the best and as long as I am alive I will work my fingers to the bone to give it to you. Just continue to always represent and respect yourself as a woman is supposed to that's all I ask of you and I will proceed to cater you spoil you just the way you like it.

Please understand my chocolate girl we've spent precious years establishing our bond love and family and we must not let anyone or anything destroy it not even our own selfishness we have experienced good and bad but now we are at that stage where we must only have the greatest love affair of all. I can hope and pray you cherish me as much as I cherish you my beautiful chocolate girl.

Until The Room Is Full Of Steam And Our Bodies Are Hot And Wet:

As we lay here together about to engross in a love affair touching one another in a pleasant way getting the mood right I plans to take you to ecstasy,

You begin to kiss my naked body in all the right places and I in return start to kiss your body in all the correct spots causing an instant heat wave to flow through the room,

I want to taste your pleasing surprise so sweet and delightful as we make love all through the night;

Do as you please and move atop of me easily let the sexy freak come out of you I want to see what the freak in you is all about so don't hold back or be shy get sassy talk to me real nasty you know how that turns me on,

Your love is powerful enough to start an earthquake I want to feel your lips blow upon my horn until it causes my body to shake;

When I saw you I fell in love with you, your smile was captivating comforting me like a hot summer day after the cold winter fades away,

I encourage you to get aggressive with your love and take control you definitely know how to work you thing the way you make love to me is so exquisite feel the fire generate through our bodies as I lick your breast you're so scrumptious, voluptuous and delicious I'm hypnotized by the way you bounce your rump on my magic wand as it goes deeper into your lovely pond;

With you, I see I have do this right stay on my A game keep on my P's and Q's I want you to get wild my sexy young girl your current may be strong, but I have the power to control your fuse, I can see the sparkle in your eyes as I penetrate my love into you I will be sure to have you enjoying the sound of the birds singing to the morning sunrise make your body glow love you slow and let the pleasure of making love flow through the air like a flock of blue birds.

I can't explain how you excite me all I know is your touch I cannot resist your my gift from God you delight me and ignite me it turns me on the way you softly bite me, it's only right that I give you a premonition before I put your sexy ass in this freaky position.

And fill you with my love potion, my actions will be sure to sooth your soul and give you satisfaction as we elaborate our bond. Feel me saturate your warm tender body, the way you whisper my name as I push deeper inside you causes me to move faster and faster like a locomotive train, hold on tight baby because this ride is not over it has only just begun and I won't stop until the room is full of steam and our bodies are hot and wet.

Touch Yourself

As we engage in a conversation over the phone I ask her how her day has been, she responds it was good but I am missing you something terrible, and I cannot wait until you return home so I can love you down and make you feel good. I tell her don't stress I will be back in about a day or two and I miss you as well and I want to hold her in my arms and kiss her sweet lips and make love to her.

She begins to tell me she is lying on the bed naked and her nipples are incredibly hard and she wishes I was there to lick on them because she is feeling so lonely. She proceeds to tell me if I was there exactly what the two of us would be doing and how she would enjoy teasing and pleasing me and all the places she wants her lips to touch me.

I respond to her saying since you are feeling hot and bothered touch yourself she giggles and says where do you want me to start I tell her surprise me she tells me she is touching her inner thighs and she is slowly rubbing her hand up and down her Vagina and its getting wet.

I then tell her to lick her nipples and squeeze them just the way I do she laughs and says not even I can pleasure myself like you do Daddy I tell her I know but I am enjoying the phone sex so she tells me to play with myself until I cum actually she then says lets both make ourselves cum.

We both now are telling one another how bad we want to feel each other she tells me she is truly horny and wetter than ever I tell her to imagine my face and tongue enjoying her juices she begins to moan and breathe heavier telling me to stroke my dick faster and make it cum. I tell her I can feel it about to cum she says me to daddy I'm about to climax she's pushing her toy deeper inside of her sweet pond smiling on the other end of the phone I tell her to turn on her side as if I were behind her and squeeze her legs together and go deeper while I am stroking my dick with great pleasure she tells me it's fun to touch herself and she cannot wait to engage in some mind blowing amazing sex once I return home her seductive words instantly causes me to bust a nut she softly says you did it daddy you came I said yes more than you would believe she laughs and says well let me cum she says I want to suck your fat dick and feel it in my ass as she continues to finger herself she says ooh daddy I am almost there.

She is breathing heavier and faster she says talk dirty to me baby I tell her how I want to spank her juicy ass and run my tongue up and down her body and lick her phat ass and fuck her from the back and in every position I can think of I ask her do you like that bad girl she say damn daddy I love it and suddenly she screams through the phone oh shit my pussy is squirting ooh ooh I am Cumming oh shit I came for you daddy and it felt so good to pleasure myself along with your assistance.

*The best part of the night is when you and I lay down
And fall asleep in each other's arms safe away from all
Of our fears and worries just you and bound together as one*

*There is no better feeling than to be locked in love with you
My sweet Angel.*

*Nothing but hugs and kisses I give to you for a life time
You are and always will be my soul mate to share love with
You is truly a pleasure a gift from God is what you are.
I'm proud to say that you are all mine.*

*The best part of the night is when you and I lay down
And fall asleep in each other's arms safe away from all
Of our fears and worries just you and bound together as one*

*There is no better feeling than to be locked in love with you
My sweet Angel.*

*Nothing but hugs and kisses I give to you for a life time
You are and always will be my soul mate to share love with
You is truly a pleasure a gift from God is what you are.
I'm proud to say that you are all mine.*

www.ingramcontent.com/pod-product-compliance
Lightning Source LLC
Chambersburg PA
CBHW042003150426
43194CB00002B/115